eel soothed ⚬ bask in beauty ⚬ receive cleansing ⚬ leave invigorated

join me at the spa ❧ be refreshed ❧ absorb pleasure ❧ enjoy hearing

spa treatments
for your body and soul

Niki,
Praying for
you! ♡
— Suss

TRANQUIL MOMENTS
TO REFRESH
YOUR SPIRIT

janie seltzer

HARVEST HOUSE PUBLISHERS

EUGENE, OREGON

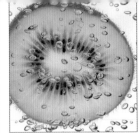

Spa Treatments for Your Body and Soul

Copyright © 2008 by Janie Seltzer
Published by Harvest House Publishers
Eugene, Oregon 97402
www.harvesthousepublishers.com

ISBN-13: 978-0-7369-2277-7
ISBN-10: 0-7369-2277-6

Design and production by Rachel Close

Printed in China

08 09 10 11 12 13 14 15 16 / LP / 10 9 8 7 6 5 4 3 2 1

To my husband, Don,
who never stopped believing

&

To Sally, who joined me in the
journey of the hidden life.

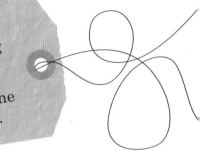

CONTENTS

cultivate a quiet mind,
find the peace that
swallows find.
widen the range of your
heart's desire,
acquire a taste for
holy things—

Remain.

join me at the spa...

For many of us, just the thought of an hour-long body massage, a cleansing facial, a pedicure, or an exotic citrus body scrub sends us into a state of relaxation and longing. Most of us are stretched and pulled to the limit, and our bodies benefit tremendously when we receive a little pampering. The challenge, however, is finding the time and/or the money to do what we need to do to live life at our best.

So the question is, how do we take care of ourselves? Even more important, how do we care for the whole person—body and soul—in today's hectic world? The body can be pampered and soothed, but if the spirit is not at peace, the benefits of an hour-long massage soon evaporate.

Within a stone's throw of my home is the world-renowned La Costa Resort and Spa. People travel from all over the globe to enjoy the lush grounds abundant with giant palms, the colorful flower beds, and the quiet simplicity of whitewashed Spanish architecture accented with red-tile roofs and black decorative ironwork. The pleasant sound of water rippling over multiple tiers of majestic terra-cotta fountains adorned with classic blue and white Mexican tiles sets the stage for an incredibly relaxing spa experience.

For Christmas this year several friends went in together to give me a gift certificate for the La Costa Spa. What a great gift! I had enjoyed the spa once before and relished the opportunity to go again. This time my plan was to spend the whole day benefiting from all of the amenities available within the enclave of the restful environment. What

I wanted—even more than the whirlpool, the cedar sauna, the steam room, the thundering Roman falls—was the quiet and tranquility of the ladies' lounge. I wanted to read, to think, to pray.

I arrived on *my day* and eagerly approached the desk to check in, only to find out that the spa was full due to a business conference crowd.

"Please don't do this to me," I said quietly to the lady at the desk.

"I am so sorry, but I cannot let you go in. There aren't any lockers available," she said.

"I don't need a locker," I persisted. "Could I please just go in and enjoy reading and writing in a quiet corner?"

"There are no quiet corners," she replied.

"Please don't do this to me. Tomorrow is my birthday."

She paused for a moment and then motioned to the girl beside her. "Let her in."

I reached for my gift certificate and handed it to the lady behind the register.

"No," she said, shaking her head. "No charge."

I was astonished and overjoyed as I entered the spa. The ladies' lounge was almost empty (go figure!), and I settled happily into a comfortable stuffed chair with a perfect view of the fireplace. While I read and relaxed, I watched women flow in and out of the lounge from nearby rooms pampered with massages, facials, and body scrubs. I watched them sink into cozy, pillow-soft sofas around the fireplace, idly thumb through magazines, or talk quietly among themselves. Suddenly I was riveted by the thought that the spa experience is a perfect parallel to the care of the spirit and the soul—and oh, how much more important!

Years ago I learned the secret of the inner spa experience. During a difficult stretch of intense challenges, loss, and deep sorrow, I learned to attend to my soul and listen to the Spirit of God as never before. I was comforted, instructed, strengthened, and nourished by the living God. I received *more* than what I had before.

I found a rich,

inner spa of life—

a constant source that continues

to this day.

In short, I found the

astonishing hidden life.

It is my hope and prayer that this book will inspire you to move in deeper, nearer to the heart of God—finding the spa of life that is always available and affordable. If you go there with the same determination that I did to spend a day at the spa for my birthday, you will never fail to find refreshment, hope, and encouragement—and all free for the taking!

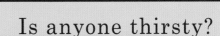

Is anyone thirsty?

Come and drink—even if you have
no money! Come, take your choice of
wine or milk—it's all free!
Why spend your money on food that
does not give you strength?
Why pay for food that
does you no good?
Listen, and I will tell you where to get
food that is good for the soul!
Come to me with your ears wide open.

LISTEN,

for the life of your soul is at stake.

Isaiah 55:1-3

I will

REFRESH THE WEARY

& satisfy the faint.

Jeremiah 31:25 NIV

be refreshed

is as refreshing to the soul as a day at a spa for the body. How amazing would it be to experience an inner landscape as alive and rejuvenated as your body feels after a massage, or as fresh as your face feels after a cucumber scrub? Better still—imagine yourself with the gift of an entire day at a world-class spa where all five senses of your body—sight, sound, smell, touch, and taste—are impacted by your experience. So it is and more when your spirit connects to the Spirit of the living God.

12

Life in the presence of God is life at its best. Nothing in our circumstances may change—though often things *do* change when we are in step with His Spirit—yet the radiance of God's love within warms, strengthens, comforts, and satisfies our deepest longings.

Are you someone who longs to be truly
REFRESHED?

While a spa treatment definitely refreshes for the length of time you are receiving it, *deep within* you know you need more in order to deal with the demands of a life filled with checklists, anxieties, and constant challenges.

Maybe, like me, you were hit by a devastating whirlwind of circumstances that threw your whole life upside down. You wonder if anything will ever be the same again.

Even a day at a spa cannot heal your soul.

Once, on a plane returning home to San Diego after a court case involving a family member, I pressed my face against the window beside me, stared out into the sky for a long time, and finally whispered this faint prayer in my soul, *God, if You are who You say You are...You have to help me...I feel dead inside. Please...help me.*

No flash of lightning streaked through the sky. No angel suddenly appeared. The plane continued on course. But I know I was heard. Slowly, steadily things began to change. Small rays of hope crept into my soul like streaks of early morning light that creep under closed doors and around the edges of closed curtains. Gradually life flowed as the love of God refreshed me, encouraged me, and surprised me in unexpected ways. In time I was able to *do life* with energy and enthusiasm again. All of the heartache did not go away, but I found safety and refuge to sustain me and even propel me forward. I did not remain stuck in my sorrow and loss.

A WORLD-CLASS SPA IS OPEN TO YOU.

You don't have to pay for it and
no one deserves it.
It is an unconditional gift from
the Creator of the universe.
He invites you in.

you are

invited

COME ON IN...

Body Treatments

essentials for a refreshing bath

Refresh your body at the end of a long day with a relaxing bubble bath.
A leisurely hot bath will help you sleep better as you unwind from the
day and wash away stress. Here are a few suggestions to get the most
enjoyment:

- Use candlelight instead of overhead lights to set a tranquil
  mood.

- Add five to ten drops of essential oils into the warm water:
    Myrrh—for overall emotional well-being.
    Rose of Sharon—to calm the nerves.
    Frankincense—to strengthen the immune system.

- Play soft instrumental music.

- Turn off your cell phone.

- Use a bath pillow or hand towel to lean your head against.

Enjoy a few minutes of personal relaxation as you *exhale*—letting go of
the worries and cares of the day—and *inhale* gratitude for another day of
life and the opportunity to rest.

In silence
HE SPEAKS—
living, moving Words
erase the bounds
of time and space,
whispers grace...
releases space
to live beyond
here and now.
*The heart flames
and sustains*
for another day.

YOU WILL SHOW ME
the way of life,
granting me the joy of
your presence

AND THE PLEASURES
of living with you
FOREVER.

······························

Psalm 16:11

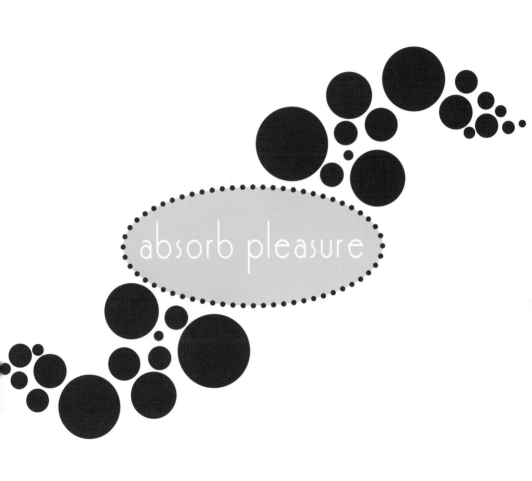

absorb pleasure

THE SPA EXPERIENCE SPELLS pleasure

It is the smell of finely perfumed candles wafting through the air. It is fountains bubbling against the backdrop of calm and inspiring music. It is elegance and orderliness, cleanliness and shine, comfortable chairs and crisp green apples in wooden bowls, and lemon water with a sprig of fresh mint to enjoy at will. All of that—even without a strawberry body buff or a stone body polish—is worth the visit!

Years ago the basic teaching of the Bible was put into a question-and-answer format called "catechism" to enable young and old to grasp the overall meaning. The first question of the catechism is:

What is the chief end of man? The answer is:

To glorify God and enjoy Him forever.

Glorify and *enjoy*...I don't think most people have wrapped their minds around enjoying God. But I believe that if they did, they would find themselves glorifying Him as well. Isn't it true that when we enjoy the company of someone, we want to get along with them and help make the relationship strong? The same is true with knowing God. Most people do not seem to grasp the concept that knowing God is pleasure—in fact, the deepest pleasure on earth.

God is not impersonal or unreachable. Quite the opposite, really. Our human personality is derived from a personal, relational Creator God who created us to love us. *Think of it:* the Creator of the universe created us in His own image—with a finely tuned spiritual and mental capacity—so that we could *enjoy* a relationship with Him.

I find great pleasure in knowing God. In His presence I find joy and peace, safety and rest, tranquility and radiance more astonishing than a summer sunset over the Pacific Ocean. In addition, I experience the pleasure of His friendship that does not go away when the sun goes down or when dark clouds roll in. In fact, I have found it to be true that when the storm rolls in He is "close to the brokenhearted" (Psalm 34:18).

"Friendship with God?" you say. Absolutely. Abraham, father of the Judeo-Christian faith, was called a friend of God. Later we are told that God would speak to Moses "as a man speaks to his friend" (Exodus 33:11). Centuries later, Jesus said, "Greater love has no one than this, that he lay down his life for his friends," and that He had taught *His friends* everything that He learned from the Father (John 15:13-15).

The pleasure of the presence of God is available to anyone who wishes to know Him, to receive His love, to honor and trust Him as God. There is so much pleasure to be found!

inhale...

THE SWEET AROMA OF THE PRESENCE OF GOD

imagine...

THE ASTONISHING PLEASURE OF FRIENDSHIP WITH GOD

Body Treatments

the pleasure of a good night's sleep

Getting enough sleep makes a huge difference in our ability to absorb pleasure. Establish a bedtime routine that signals rest to your mind and your body. Just as children respond best to a predictable routine in settling down for the night, we adults need to signal to our own bodies that it's time to wind down.

Train yourself to settle in to a good night's sleep by following the same pattern each night and going to bed at about the same time. Sipping herbal tea or a cup of hot milk before you go to bed is a good way to unwind. Or try a cup of low-fat yogurt with fresh berries before lying down.

Avoid alcohol, coffee, rousing conversations, and intense television or reading. Turn on soft music and choose light reading material to take your thoughts off the day's activities and calm your mind. As your eyelids start to get heavy and your mind drifts off, turn out the light and cozy up to the comforting peace of a good night's sleep. Your complexion and your whole body will thank you.

Leave room for God
to come;
SURPRISING PRESENCE
AND POWER—
at your right or left.
Be still, and wait…celebrate
the good *pleasure*
of His company.

LET ME *hear*
of your unfailing love
to me in the morning,
FOR I AM TRUSTING YOU.

Psalm 143:8

enjoy hearing

Hearing from God
IS WHAT MAKES YOUR RELATIONSHIP
PERSONAL

The hushed tones of a spa reflect the same kind of conditions that enable us to hear God—who speaks in hushed tones deep within our souls.

L I S T E N
the voice is small,
s t i l l
whispers of truth
to the timid will.
real it comes,
trust the love—
a dove of wonder
hovers,
D I S C O V E R !

To hear God we need to find a place where we can escape the noises of our world. Everyone can find a quiet place, or at least a private place, if they try. A mentor of mine once said that *we all do what we want to do*—and for many years and in many different circumstances I have found she was right. An even bigger challenge is quieting the noises within our anxious minds.

I like to think of the mental clutter as yellow chicks:

> In solitude, I gather up
> all the loose ends of my soul
> like yellow chicks that scurry
> and flurry in all directions.
> I gather each one and tuck them
> under my wings where they must
> wait to be reordered according to
> some grand scheme that I cannot see
> and do not know
> but works when I trust
> AND FOLLOW IT.

29

Hearing from God is worth the effort. Our restless and frazzled minds are soothed in the presence of God as we read and listen to His Word. The Bible is a love letter to us. Open it and read. You will find truth to live by. You will find encouragement and grace as soothing as an amazing head massage administered by loving, skillful hands... *shhhhhhh*...listen.

escape
the noises of our world
YOU WILL FIND TRUTH TO LIVE BY

seek

solitude

Body Treatments

the benefits of meditative moments

Studies show that when you spend at least 20 minutes a day in quiet meditation, you experience a relaxation response that results in lower blood pressure and better concentration throughout the day. The benefits of daily stillness with God hold treasure for your life that is surprising. Sacred space—a quiet time to meet with God—is essential for growth in your spiritual life. Here are the basics:

show up...Find a comfortable and quiet place of solitude for personal worship and meditation.

wake up...If you start your day with God, wake up with a cup of coffee or tea. Focus your mind and inwardly turn your heart to God.

look up...Begin by reading a scripture-based devotional and/or a daily Bible. (My favorite: just turn to the day.) Time permitting, read the passage *once* to grasp the overall meaning, *twice* to take in the details, and a *third* time to personalize. Write down your thoughts and prayers in a journal.

listen up...Be alert to the presence of God: "Draw close to God, and God will draw close to you" (James 4:8). Listen for the whispers of the Spirit. Be patient with yourself as you learn to listen.

lift up...Freely express the needs and desires of your heart and the needs of others. One way to end is to say the Lord's Prayer slowly, personally: *My Father in heaven, so holy is your name...* (Matthew 6:9-13).

I need to hear, Father.
I SLIP INTO YOUR PRESENCE
s h e d d i n g
senseless noise that overpowers
and disrupts my hearing.

I am listening, Father.
I ATTEND TO THE YEARNING
that lives and hungers
for more of You.

Thank You for speaking, Father.
YOU SPEAK LIVING WORDS
and fill sacred space that is secret
hidden, intimate–and eternal.

peace I leave with you

Peace I leave with you;
my peace I give you.
I DO NOT GIVE TO YOU AS THE WORLD GIVES.
Do not let your hearts be troubled and do not be afraid.

do not be afraid

John 14:27 NIV

34

feel soothed

The spa experience speaks to our bodies and spirits so profoundly because the serenity and safety we find there helps to soothe our nerves. Fear is a constant battle for all of us.

We often feel vulnerable in this world—and the truth is we are vulnerable.

We humans are more like sheep than any other creature in God's Kingdom. The Scriptures regularly use the analogy of sheep to shepherd to describe our relationship with God. There are many reasons for that—and one of the most important is that sheep cannot protect themselves from wild animals. They need a shepherd to protect and care for them. The shepherd carries a big stick or rod to defend the sheep from wolves and other animals that move in to attack.

Also, sheep will not drink from running water; they need quiet, placid pools. The shepherd will go to great lengths to find calm, peaceful water. Only then will the sheep drink.

As with sheep, agitation and anxiety are like poison to our souls and our bodies. When we are tied up in knots, we can't think clearly, make wise decisions, or enjoy the day or our life. Our health is destroyed by worry and fear. Sometimes fear is so powerful that our life is limited and controlled by it.

There is no doubt about it: a massage, facial, or even a pedicure can do much to temporarily relieve stress. *Oh, yes!* However, what we need even more is treatment that goes deeper than the skin. We need true inner calm for our spirit.

When I was a college student at UNC Chapel Hill, I went through an unexpected battle with a fear that seemed to come out of nowhere. After months of not knowing where to turn, I finally marched to my dorm room (in the middle of a beautiful, Carolina blue sky day), locked my door, got down on my knees, and had a serious conversation with God. *Why am I so afraid?*

In the end I did find freedom from the fear. I learned that my true security is in God alone. I learned what it means to trust. The experience has resonated positively in my life for the last 30 years. These words from the psalmist truly became my words: "I prayed to the LORD, and he answered me, freeing me from all my fears" (Psalm 34:4).

What I suggest you do to begin to deal with your fears and anxieties—so much a part of the human condition—is to bask in the soothing atmosphere of God's presence. Begin to turn your inner eyes to Jesus—the one who "even the wind and waves obey" (Mark 4:41). He has the power to give peace to your spirit. *Ask Him...*He is the prince of peace. He can help you breathe deeply and think freely.

His love can heal you and fill you.

THE POWER OF
divine love overcomes
FEAR.

Believe me—your soul will be soothed and
your life will take on a new freedom.

Do not be

afraid

Body Treatments

create a soothing lifestyle

A few simple changes in your lifestyle can reap big rewards toward a more soothing, less frantic life.

try these...

- Wake up 30 minutes earlier so that you don't have to rush into your day. Begin your day calm, not frantic. Welcome God into your day and then ask for His help.

- Use a day planner (digital or paper) to store your to-dos and info.

- Schedule rest and play time. Learn to say no sometimes to give yourself down time.

- Designate a place to keep your car keys and other essentials and keep them there.

- Minimize your paper clutter by filing what is important and throwing away what's not.

- Simplify and organize your environment.

- Make time once a week to escape the busyness of your life and have lunch, dinner—or just a cup of coffee or tea—with a good friend. Life is short; take time for what really matters.

Lord of love, soothe my heart;
STEADY THE TREMBLING, LISTLESS SWELLS
and rise in the power of Your peace.
THEN FEAR, FLEE! AND, I
in Your Presence—Serene.

41

One thing I ask of the LORD,
THIS IS WHAT I SEEK:
that I may dwell in the
house of the LORD
ALL THE DAYS OF MY LIFE,
to gaze upon the
beauty of the LORD
and to seek him in his temple.

Psalm 27:4 NIV

bask in beauty

BEAUTY REFRESHES & FEEDS THE SPIRIT. When you enter a lovely, serene spa, watch the sun rise or set, sit by the ocean and watch the waves roll in, listen to an uplifting song, walk through an art gallery, stroll through an elegant garden, or hike along an untouched trail—your spirit is somehow strengthened and energized. Why is that?

Often, when my spirit is limp, sad, or overwhelmed, I retreat to the Batiquitos Lagoon near my home. I find great comfort in the natural beauty as I walk along the earthen path that winds around the tranquil water surrounded by tall grassy marshes that sway in the cool breeze flowing off the nearby Pacific Ocean. Eucalyptus trees are home to graceful white egrets and majestic blue herons, which chatter among themselves. The scent of wild licorice and honeysuckle permeates the air, and the cheerful spots of yellow mustard and daisy wildflowers dash the landscape here and there. Sometimes I disappear into a hidden grove of trees close to the water where I hide just to be still, listen, and absorb the beauty. God is near in

the cool of this private refuge. Mysteriously, my spirit sinks and then soars as egrets lift off the water and then dip into the lagoon for their evening meal.

Have you ever considered that God Himself is beautiful? His beauty totally captivates me. Each day when I seek Him, I find beauty, light, and hope—even when the sky is gray (not too often in San Diego!) or my day is filled with enormous responsibility or weighted with worries. The light of God enlivens my soul.

External circumstances do not have to dictate our mood. Of course, tragedy and heartache do happen, and the impact is disorienting and often terrible. But aside from the riveting events of life, ordinary days can be filled with beauty through the connection made through God's Spirit. All of life is touched. Healing happens. Attitudes shift. Eyes brighten with beauty.

My sense is that we are drawn and fed by beauty due to our hunger and thirst for the divine. The Scriptures tell us God has planted eternity in the human heart (Ecclesiastes 3:11). All of us know, deep in our core, that our real home is someplace else...and beauty calls us there.

gaze upon

turn
your heart to
simple things,

alert
to spots of
beauty,

seek
the spectrum of the
Light—

and go—
most of all, to God
so bright,
so bright!

the beauty

Body Treatments

the benefits of beauty

Enhancing the beauty of your personal space gives a lift to your attitude and your energy. Just a dash of color makes an immense difference. Yellow warms and speaks optimism. Red resonates with power and energy. Blue calms and whispers tranquility. Green soothes and heals.

Bring beauty into your life with
COLOR, SCENTS, AND TOUCHES OF LOVE.

- Add a bright bouquet of flowers or live, potted plants.

- Create a fresh look in a room by painting one wall a vibrant color.

- Add the fresh scent of aromatic candles.

- Strategically position photos of people you love.

- Rearrange your space to be pleasing to the eye by grouping like objects. Odd numbers of things are the most interesting.

- Add a touch of your favorite color with a few scatter pillows.

Beauty

TOUCHES THE HEART

when Jesus comes,

LIFTS INTO FLIGHT

what's lost in deep night

LOVES INTO LIFE

quiets strife

MAKES EYES BRIGHT.

HAVE MERCY ON ME,
O God,
because of your unfailing
LOVE.

BECAUSE OF YOUR
great compassion,
blot out the stain of my
SINS.

WASH ME CLEAN
from my guilt.

PURIFY ME
from my sin.

Psalm 51:1-2

receive cleansing

PERVADES THE SPA ENVIRONMENT

The luxurious white robe you put on when you first enter a spa sets the tone. One of the amenities of my local spa is a *free* body scrub. Oh my, love the scrub! After the scrub I get to choose if I want lavender, citrus, or vanilla water spritzed over my cleansed skin. *Sooo nice.*

Freshness, cleanliness, wholeness—all that is healthy surrounds you. You feel better just being there. You wish you could live like this all the time!

We can.

In fact, we can do better. We can have freshness that radiates from the inside out by wearing the beautiful robe of forgiveness. A key word to understand is "atonement." "Atone" means "to make amends." Atonement removes all barriers between us and God.

We all have barriers. These walls prevent us from accessing all that is available in God. Maybe you long to indulge in the Lord but sense you cannot break through… Maybe, just maybe, what you need is an inner cleansing and forgiveness for those things you have done and said that grieve the Holy Spirit of God. An inner scrub, if you will.

It is so doable! God Himself has made it possible and has the scrub ready and waiting. All you have to do is ask for it...*just ask*. Ask for forgiveness and *receive the free gift*. Jesus made amends for you—broke down the barriers—when He died on the cross. He paid for our sins with His suffering. It's hard to believe, but it's true. And—He knew you by name. In fact, He knew you before He created the world.

Don't be afraid to enter into the spa with your

IMPURITIES.

That's what a spa is for!

Think about it—you come in exhausted, with clogged pores and sore muscles, you come out refreshed, cleansed, and strengthened. Ah, the freshness you will feel when you let God cleanse you! It is more wonderful than a deep cleansing facial or an orange blossom body scrub...indulge.

freshness

ALL YOU HAVE TO DO IS ASK...JUST ASK

cleanliness

wholeness

Body Treatments
suggestions for a great home facial

You can pamper and cleanse your face by purchasing a deep cleansing facial mask at any local drugstore or beauty supply. Then...

follow these steps:

- Slice a cucumber (save the leftovers for a fresh crisp salad later).
- Fasten back your hair and wash your face thoroughly.
- Apply the mask according to directions.
- Turn on peaceful music.
- Lie down in a comfortable position. Place the cucumbers on your eyes and relax.
- When the mask begins to harden—cleansing your pores—maintain your stillness for the allotted period of time.
- Splash your face with warm water to remove the mask.
- Apply a moisturizer and bask in the glow of your freshly cleansed and healthy skin!

Or, for a ten-minute luxury facial, start with a cleansed face, then combine coconut oil and fine sea salt and in a circular motion gently massage your face for two to three minutes. Rinse with a wet warm washcloth. Tone and moisturize your skin with products containing essential oils and fruit acids.

Holy Father
clear the cobwebs and corners of my soul
WHERE DARKNESS DWELLS.

Crush the rush of sin within my veins—
A world competes, with eerie enticements,

57

And enemies abound.
SHINE, SHINE THE CLEANSING TRUTH
Your Word contains, and there

{Remain.}

I have come
THAT THEY MAY HAVE LIFE,
and have it to the full.

John 10:10 NIV

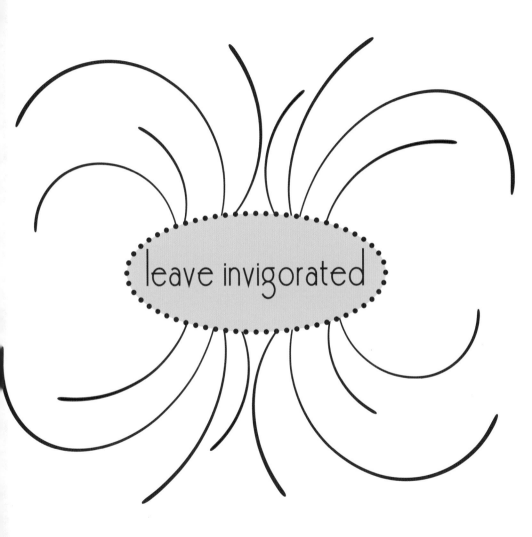

leave invigorated

One of the secrets of the spa is

THE BEAUTY OF SOLITUDE.

Even if you're in the company of a friend, you can enjoy your own pace and your own space. You can breathe. You speak only if you wish. No pressure. Relax…and BE.

You cannot become all you can be without solitude. Solitude opens wide the doors and windows to wonder. Wonder works its way through your whole being like the kneading of gentle hands massaging fine oil into your body.

You become present to yourself; you become present to God. Someone calls your name and you answer: "Here I am." Then, as you are present to yourself, fully in the moment, slowly you become present to God. The two work hand in hand.

The wonderful gift you find is *real presence* in solitude, not emptiness. More presence than you ever imagined. Once tasted, the sweetness becomes your longing. The day is flat without it. And all of this by giving yourself to the environment.

In a spa you surrender to the solitude of the spa—follow the procedure, relax in the vulnerability—allow someone safe to lead the way in massaging the body, cleansing the face, scrubbing the pores, filing the nails. Surrender, in circumstances where safety dwells, invigorates.

Jesus, the Good Shepherd, asks for that same kind of surrender. *Follow Me; I will take you where you need to go. I know the way. You are safe with Me. I will not lead you astray. I will never abandon you. I am going to show you real life. Take My hand. Let Me lead.*

Each person, alone, needs to take His hand. This is not the time to look around and see what others are doing. He speaks personally. He asks, *Is there anything more important than the soul?*

If we follow, trust, let go, and let Him lead—we find a whole new way of life that can be replenished regularly in His presence. We find a faithful lover of our soul. We find invigoration, wisdom, strength, and peace. Surrender to God brings joy to the spirit.

Try it. He is safe.

It is my hope and prayer that you will join me in the spa.

Remember—*it's free.*

Come on in...

IT'S YOUR BIRTHDAY.

Find the secret of being alive

Practice God's presence
Get into His stride.
Choose a place—private
Be still in your soul;
Soak in the silence...
In time you'll be whole.

Lift up in earnest

the simple Lord's prayer;
Walk through it
slowly,
Instruction is there.

Speak to the Father;

Watch humbly for Jesus.
He promised His presence
And never to leave us.

For more on the beauty
of a life hidden in Christ, visit

www.hiddenlife.com

join me at the spa ✤ be refreshed ✤ absorb pleasure ✤ enjoy hearing